REPENTANCE:

THE POWER

OF

FORGIVENESS

Vol. II

By Dr. Antonio B. Jones, CPM

No part of this work may be reproduced or transmitted in any form or by any means, electronic or mechanical, including photocopying and recording, or by any information storage retrieval system without the prior written permission of the author & JMI Enterprises, LLC, unless such copying is expressly permitted by federal copyright law.

Address inquiries to
JMI International
Attn: Administrator
P.O. Box 8092
Fayetteville, NC 28311
www.jonesministries.org

First Edition
Printed in the U.S.A.
Copyright © JMI Enterprises, LLC
All rights reserved.

All Greek Definitions taken from
The Greek Online Concordance
http://www.biblos.com

All scripture quoted from The Authorized King James Version
(Unless otherwise noted)

Cover Image: Veronica Wilkinson

Purposed2Design.com

Typeset in Arial Unicode MS

Font size for this book is increased to accommodate those with visual impairments.

FOREWORD

I first give GOD ALL THE GLORY for this book and the others that will follow. I am nothing and cannot do anything without my FATHER.

The contents of the Forgiveness Series comprise a series of messages revelated to Apostle Jones during an unspecified period of time. As directed by God, this book series does not have a traditional flow as the information outlined throughout the book is as God revealed them and in "spiritual order" per the direction of the Spirit of God.

Hence, it is intended to be read from the very beginning without the customary "table of contents browsing" that allows one to choose where to begin, in hopes of getting to the "good stuff." God gave the contents of this book, so it is ALL GOOD because it is ALL GOD!!

This series as well as the other books, devotionals,

etc. that God instructed Dr. Jones to begin to release, will not follow the traditional and/or industry standards established. God has ordained Apostle Jones to write as HE instructed as well as in the manner in which to write, to include, but not limited to, actual dialogues from prayer and/or meditation sessions and immediate revelation that God reveals during the actual typing of the manuscripts.
God has called Apostle Jones to be a pioneer, a type of forerunner that will do EXACTLY what HE says, even if the world says it is not the best way or the customary way to do it.

So in the spirit of totally obedient and excellence in spirit, Dr. Jones has begun to release some of the most prolific, insightful, as well as practical material this generation has ever seen.

We challenge you to open your mind in order to fully receive what God desire to impart into you through the various publications of Apostle Jones. Utilize what is applicable to you and/or your situations and allow GOD to reveal the rest to you.

As you read this book and others by Dr. Jones, we ask that you read it with the intent of receiving what GOD desires for you to, not for the text style, format, etc.
God works in various ways and the publications from God written by Dr. Jones is just one way God chose to manifest Himself to the world.

Thank you for your continual support of our Apostle, Dr. Antonio B. Jones.

DEDICATION

This book is dedicated to my family, *Dr. Amichia S.Jones*, or *Michia*, as she is affectionately known to me, Joel Marquez, and Antonio Jairus Bernard (AJ).

All of you have been by my side since day one and have never faltered in your unyielding support of what God called me to do. You understood those long nights & early mornings and ensured that I was taken care of. As a family, we had to walk through a lot of hard times, challenging times, and times that we simply did not understand. Together, as a family, we stood together, depending solely on God, and we made it through. This second volume in the Forgiveness Series, as well as the others forthcoming, contains some of our experiences in these very same subjects that God has now released me to publish. Thank you for being unselfish and sharing revelation as each of you received it from God. I respect the God that is in each of you, the anointing that He has placed in you as well as the true support system you all are to me.

God has seen the sacrifices each of you made on HIS behalf that enabled me to fulfill what He called me to do. Be assured that HE will reward you greatly and know that He has and will continue to bless you for doing so. **Amichia,** continue to bless the world with your radiating smile, insightful books & teachings. I am honored to be your husband, co-laborer in the Gospel, and friend. I love you.

Joel and Antonio (Jairus):

You demonstrated your commitment to the completion of this book thru your obedience and by assisting your mother to help lighten the load during my long nights and mornings. You both were a constant motivation to me, always encouraging me to "GO HARD!" I love you both and it is truly an honor and privilege to have you as my sons. Your commitment to your school and AAU basketball teams were an inspiration to me as I saw how you maintained your good grades, went to practices several times a week and then performed at very high levels during your basketball games. This was in addition to your work at the local church. This was very commendable for a 15 & 13 yr. old. **Joel & Jairus**, it was through your dedication to what you believed in and your desire to excel "*by any means necessary*" that encouraged YOUR FATHER. You are the best two sons in the WORLD. I am blessed to be your father and to be an active part of your lives.   You both   "GO HARD!!"

JOEL MARQUEZ   ANTONIO JAIRUS (AJ)

REFERENCE POINTS

Introduction	12
What is Repentance	14
What is Forgiveness	18
Forgiveness in Financial Matters	26
Physical Manifestations of Forgiveness	68
MARY: A Case Study	80
Soulish Justification	92
Forgiveness Assessment	104
Vision Plan	130
Scriptures	134
Prayers	143
Conclusion: Points to Ponder	148
Ministry Information	164

INTRODUCTION

The Bible clearly informs us that trials and tribulations will come our way, even more so for Believers. One reason the aforementioned comes our way is to test our faith and to ensure that our lives, belief systems, etc., are built upon the foundation of Christ. *Matthew 7:24-27* provides our scriptural basis as to why building upon a solid foundation is so important, hence why God released me now to discuss repentance and forgiveness in a practical yet simple manner. Why the foundation of repentance and forgiveness? Well, God will test our submission to Him as our personal Lord & savior. We demonstrate our submission through our obedience to His word, not just knowing His word (scripture). Being part of God's family, we must know about such basic or foundational things such as repentance and forgiveness.

Naturally speaking, there are things, accomplishments, etc., that you parents, grandparents, etc. have passed on to you that are very specific to your family. Some, if not all of these things, provided a foundation for what you have done, are doing, and what you have or will become. So just as we experience things in life, our experience with the foundational things of Christ, help us make the transition to becoming the new creature *(II Cor.5:17)* after we receive salvation.

Therefore, our experiences with and learning foundational truths, such as forgiveness & repentance, better prepare us to face future tests, trials, and tribulations. If we are to really grow and mature in the things of God, we must learn & apply foundational truths so that we will be able to do just that, Grow Up!

Let us begin with a recap of Volume I.

WHAT IS REPENTANCE

DEFINITION: Repentance is a radical change of mind and heart, which comes about from seeing your true spiritual state in the light of God's Holiness and perfection, which results on a total change of direction. It is a literal about face from sin as well as dead works to our living God which subsequently results in a TOTAL change of life (attitude, behavior, responses, etc.). It involves:

1. Accepting God's holy attitude to sin and rebellion
2. Seeing yourself as personally guilty of that rebellion
3. Confessing this personally

4. Obeying God's call to turn from that life of sin and self and to receive forgiveness.

5. A change of mind, which results in a turning around, to face and move in the opposite direction.

Throughout the New Testament, the Greek word "Metanoein" is translated " to repent." This word has one meaning throughout all the history of Greek both in classical Greek and New Testament Greek. Its basic meaning is "to change one's mind "/ The Old Testament Hebrew brings out a slightly different meaning - it literally means to "turn to "return" or to "turn back". Put the two together and you have a perfect picture of Repentance.

The inward change of mind <u>must be accompanied by the outward change of direction.</u>
In short, you turn AWAY from the world and TOWARDS God. You begin your Christian journey of living by faith, walking by faith, believing that with GOD all things are possible, and begin being a

living, walking, example of God here on earth by demonstrating His love, compassion, and power.

Acts 3:19 - "Repent in order that your sins may be blotted out."

To ask God to forgive you for being a rebel and yet remain a rebel is unthinkable. You cannot ask God to take you back without actually going back. This is hypocritical in every sense of the word.

If you have repented, you are now in a position to ask and receive from God all that He wants to give. Yes! God does WANT to give you things, to bless you, to sustain you. You are his child and just as a natural father or mother cares for and provides needs & desires, so does our God. This is why repentance is not only an initial turning around from a self-determining, self-centered life, but a continual and constant attitude of heart so that whenever God puts His finger on sin and selfishness in our lives, our instant response is one of repentance –

maturing from just being sorry to being able to stop the behavior(s) that led us to repentance.

It is important to know that repentance ALWAYS begins with God.

Read *John 6:44*, *Lamentations 5:21*, and *Psalms 80:3; 7:19* to see this in scripture.

Forgiveness is what follows true repentance. One cannot have true forgiveness without repenting first. So let's take a look at what forgiveness means.

WHAT IS FORGIVENESS

DEFINITION: Forgive (verb) means;
- to grant pardon for or remission of an offense, adverse action, debt, etc.,
- to absolve;
- to give up all claim on account of;
- remit (i.e., debt, obligation, etc.);
- to grant pardon as to a person;
- to cease to feel resentment, anger, hostility, etc. against another person;
- to cancel an indebtedness or financial liability of.

Therefore, we can simply define forgiveness (noun) to mean the act of or one's willingness to forgive. A verb usually has an object which receives its action. So it is with the act of forgiving.

Someone, not something, must receive the action as stated in the definition.

To forgive, therefore, means essentially to pardon the person who committed the offense or wrongdoing and to remove the guilt resulting from the wrongdoing. We will look at the different aspects of forgiveness later in the book but to further explain the aforementioned, let's look at a few words.

There are several original Greek words that can mean forgiveness. For the purpose of this volume, I will use "aphiemi", "aphesis" and "apoluo", which all virtually mean "to remove the guilt that derived from wrongdoings".

I want to briefly focus on the meanings of 'aphiemi', 'aphesis' and 'apoluo' due to the fact that they deal primarily with the guilt of the wrongdoer and not upon the actual wrongdoing itself. Why is this important you ask? Well, when God forgives the wrongdoer aka the person that committed the offense, the actual event of wrongdoing is not undone, but, however, the guilt resulting from the action or wrongdoing is forgiven.

The same applies to us. When we forgive someone for a particular action, it does NOT mean that the action did NOT occur but rather that we are CHOOSING to forgive the person who performed the particular action.

This is a key principle because this fact alone has prevented many from actually forgiving individuals. They cannot separate the person from the action. You see, even though the actual wrongdoing did occur, with God's help, you can eliminate the pain, hurt, disappoint, and other emotions, etc. that are associated with the action, FOREVER!

This can't be possible you say? Well, it is! This is the power of FORGIVENESS made possible through God's grace and His son Jesus's shedding blood on the cross, becoming the ultimate & final sacrifice for ALL of our sins.

What am I saying? Our Lord and Saviour Jesus Christ paid the cost for forgiveness (of sins, trespasses, etc.) but it is up to us as individuals to receive this gift by doing our part in the equation, FORGIVE OTHERS! I will use the following practical & simple example to demonstrate simply what this means.

Let's say you were at a grocery store and the person in front of you informs you that they have paid for all the products you have in your basket. You get to the counter, see the cashier with the

money and he or she tells you that your purchase is already paid for.

The cashier even shows you the money again. In order for you to take your "purchased" products and/or groceries home, you would have to BELIEVE that the money you saw was real and you would have to actually RECEIVE the free gift by performing an action (putting your groceries on the conveyor belt to be rung up).

You see, although Christ has already "paid" for your ability to forgive & be forgiven, we must believe it, receive it, and consequently, act upon it. The mere fact alone that you know forgiveness is available to you is not enough.

In order for the POWER of FORGIVENESS to operate fully in your life, you must choose or will yourself to act upon it and actually use it if it is to truly and sincerely benefit you.

Anyone sincerely desiring to forgive someone must first know that it is God Himself who not only made it possible to be able to forgive but it is He who also placed the <u>desire</u> in you to do so.

As we learned in Volume I, our hearts are naturally & desperately wicked that without the Holy Spirit putting this desire in us, there would be no way that we would even remotely desire to turn to God to make forgiveness possible.

The scriptures tell us that there is nothing good in our flesh and that we were born in sin and shaped in iniquity, which means we do not have the capacity to forgive in and of ourselves. This is one of the reasons why the actual act of forgiveness is so difficult.

We were not created to forgive without the help of the sovereign God. We need him. Think about it for a moment. Some people have done some terrible things to us, our families, and others we love.

<u>Naturally</u>, we could (and do) justify why we should not forgive the person(s) who committed the act and feel fully vindicated in doing so. Our flesh is appeased, our emotions are thereby justified, and we feel a "peace" within ourselves, albeit a superficial one. I say the latter because without true

forgiveness, there really is no true peace. This is why, my friends, we need God's assistance thru His love, mercy, grace, and infinite wisdom to truly forgive.

I have to stress needing God's help because it is the only way to begin, complete, and walk in the act of forgiveness. We need God and the blood of Jesus to cleanse & purify us, from the inside out.

The Bible informs us that "*God is not willing that any should perish but that all should come to repentance.*" *(2 Pet 3:9).*

God has forgiven you so let us begin forgiving others.

FORGIVING IN FINANCIAL MATTERS

Matthew 18:27- "*Then the lord of that servant was moved with compassion, and loosed him, and gave him the debt.*"

"*It is OK to have money, but do not allow money to HAVE you.*"
Dr. Antonio B. Jones

As stated in Volume I, we will begin to look at some real life examples of forgiveness and what better way to begin this section of the book that with one of the most common areas where forgiveness is indicated, in money matters.

Eccles.5:12- "*The sleep of a labouring man is sweet, whether he eat little or much: but the abundance of the rich will not suffer (allow) him to sleep.*"

I am a firm believer in transparency and what it can do to substantiate a particular teaching so I am led to share in regards to forgiving in the area of money.

Years ago, my wife and I began to do well financially as God was continually blessing us and we were being the good stewards over that which He had blessed us with.

During this time there were some individuals who had asked to borrow a certain amount of money so that they take care of some things that had come up. We had known these people for some time now and knew that they were genuine individuals who really would not ask for assistance unless it was really needed.

This, coupled with the fact of their impeccable record of integrity up to that point, made this decision fairly easy. This aspect of integrity & character was a major contributing factor as we were very big on keeping one's word, accountability and responsibility.

My wife and I agreed to lend the money per the terms outlined by these individuals. The financial exchange took place and we were giving God glory for allowing us to even be in the place financially to assist for we knew God blesses you to be a blessing to others.

Well, as time went by so did our conversations with these individuals. That was a sign that something was not going according to what was originally stated. Not being pressed for the money or willing to loose friendship over something as temporal as money, we attributed the passing of the deadline for repayment as a simple oversight.

As more weeks and months went by without a call to share the apparent dilemma, I began to become somewhat upset. Here it was that we had loaned money to trusted friends (with a history of integrity) based on repayment terms they had formulated, which were by the way, extremely lenient. It baffled us however, that neither chose to extend a similar act of kindness or courtesy by making a simple call to us to possibly share that the terms of the repayment plan were not able to be met or that more time was needed. Wow!! I honestly thought, how dare you treat friends like that?! REALLY!!

I began to become extremely upset, agitated, and honestly, somewhat bitter against them, not because of the amount of money but rather the intentional lack of communication and seemingly betrayal of trust. I then began to tell myself that I should not have loaned the money and began thinking about how I could have used that money on other meaningful things. The old nature tried to show its ugly head and was truthfully gaining momentum from my emotions that were running wild.

I gave every space for the enemy to come in and exploit my feelings in an attempt to pull me out of acting and remaining in love.

As a Christian, I did the only thing I knew to do, GO TO GOD IN PRAYER! How many of you know that my initial "prayer" to God was really not a prayer at all but rather a gripe session with me telling God how badly my family had been treated.

After all, these people were good friends who we had done things with, shared things with and to be totally overlooked was unforgivable. I even had the audacity to foolishly ask God to allow them to "feel" something to make them call to explain or set up a time or place to give the money back.

TRUTH CHECK: How many of us have ever <u>allowed</u> anger, hurt, disappointment, etc., to cause us to either speak or desire something negative to happen to those who are responsible for our specific feeling(s)? If your answer was never, I am in prayer for you now that the spirit of deception leaves you now in the name of Jesus and that the eyes of your understanding be enlightened! Why? Because we ALL have. Me?

Yes <u>YOU</u> as well!!

It does not matter what is in front of our names nor what is behind our names, what our social status is, nor what religious persuasion we may be of. This has applied to us ALL at some point in time. Remember, part of the FORGIVENESS process is actually <u>admitting</u> that something is there, that there is something you must effectively deal with in order to even ALLOW the healing to begin.

Needless to say, my "get them God" was truly a monologue with me speaking to the air and actually not to God. I was doing all the talking, or rather complaining and telling God what I wanted to occur because I allowed my family to be hurt or adversely affected by this wrongdoing instead of asking God what was His Will in the matter.

I know you may be asking, "How was that initial prayer and feeling wrong? After all, you do have feelings also and such thoughts do come to your mind."

Albeit true, my response cannot be as such. We are instructed to anger but sin not (Eph.4:26) as true believers. Is it always easy? Definitely not! Is it still required? Yes, it is. The dilemma or challenge per se, is actually HOW to appropriate this scripture and consistently apply it to your life.

My friends, you do this by actually going "through" such situations and being very intentional in applying this principle more and more each time you experience such. I must say that with this process, you will feel like abandoning this principle but I encourage you to pull on the spirit of God inside you to stay the course or else you will never overcome what you so easily give in to. We give in so easily, it APPEARS to be a natural part of us, but it is not.

In addition, when these "natural" feelings come, we must rely on the supernatural "spirit" to help us to not reaction (per our feelings) but respond (according to God's way). How do we respond?

We respond IN LOVE and WITH the Holy Spirit. Any other way will yield less desirable results, not pleasing to our Father.

Although the feelings and emotions I was experiencing were in fact very real, I still had the responsibility as a Christian believer to apply 2 Corinthians 10:5 which reads:

"Casting down imaginations, and every high thing that exalteth itself against the knowledge of God, and bringing into captivity every thought to the obedience of Christ."

Let me re-state this per the *Message Version (v3-6):*

3-6 The world is unprincipled. It's dog-eat-dog out there! The world doesn't fight fair. But we don't live or fight our battles that way—never have and never will. The tools of our trade aren't for marketing or manipulation, but they are for demolishing that entire massively corrupt culture.

We use our powerful God-tools for smashing warped philosophies, tearing down barriers erected against the truth of God, fitting every loose thought and emotion and impulse into the structure of life shaped by Christ.

Our tools are ready at hand for clearing the ground of every obstruction and building lives of obedience into maturity.

Those thoughts that I had of revenge, bitterness and wanting them to "feel" something are classified as evil imaginations, warped philosophy that is embraced by the world and even some professionals. They were not a reason or justification to feel the way I felt but more so a reason as to why I should not feel that way; doing so shifted the power to them and rendered me helpless in regards to my own feelings, actions, and how this incident could adversely affect future actions and behaviors.

These feelings and emotions were also attempting to make themselves more important, more meaningful, more POWERFUL than the knowledge and love of God that I possessed which simply said,

"FORGIVE!"

Well, after I finished my spiritual filibuster, the majority (GOD) spoke. I am going to share what He spoke to me very simple.

God said,*" Antonio, are you finished? Is there anything else you want me to know? Is there anything else you must tell me? You know better than this. I have so much more for you to do and if you yield here, you immediately stop what I am desiring to do for you, your family, the businesses, and the ministry. I am requiring you to*

"Let it go, <u>NOW!</u>"

I was shocked but not really surprised because truth be told, I DID KNOW BETTER but I had already spoken and now I had to receive (this word from God), even though I (my flesh) didn't really want to. Now when I say flesh, I am referring to the natural part of us, our souls, and the seat of our emotions & feelings, which always has an innate desire to feel good no matter what the cost or at anyone's expense.

Yes, there are times when all of us really do not want to hear what God has to say because being one of His children, we knew what we were going to hear, exactly what we had heard from the beginning but failed to act upon!

The aforementioned should jar your memory to reflect back on how this occurred somewhere in our childhood and/or adulthood.

What I am simply saying is this; openly confess to God about these and other feelings you may experience. He did not intend for them to stay bottled up inside of you, causing ailments, sickness, and disease, which will briefly discuss in another chapter.

For me in this situation, God simply said," **FORGIVE THEM AND FORGET ABOUT THE MONEY"**.

Naturally, I said,"Do what God? THEY are the ones that told us they would repay in a certain amount of time. THEY are the ones that basically lied to us. THEY are the ones that perpetuated the wrongdoing. THEY are the ones needing to ask us forgiveness."

God gracefully answered, "And both of YOU are the ones who will forgive them and move on."

I must say this hit me like a ton of bricks. Amichia & I, forgive THEM for something that THEY did? Notice in my discourse to God how I constantly used the word "THEY." God basically was telling us, what about YOU?

You see, we cannot control what others do but we

can control what we do. You can choose to empower yourself through forgiving or empower others by failing to forgive. What do you choose?

At this point, we both honestly knew we had to forgive them but our again felt as if our feelings were "justified" because we were on the receiving end of the wrongdoing and didn't do anything to deserve to be treated like this. Listen to this; after all, we had a <u>right</u> to not forgive and to be upset. Although we had a natural right to be upset, we had a spiritual <u>right</u> & <u>obligation</u> to forgive. LOVE had to prevail.

Now, how could we <u>effectively</u> teach & minister on forgiveness if we were not operating in it ourselves? Our names were not Gilligan, the Captain, or Mary Ann (reference *Gilligan's Island* sitcom), so we were not going to be castaways as noted in *I Cor.9:27*, saying one thing but doing another. There was just one thing left to do, forgive them and release ourselves from the cruel taskmaster called UNFORGIVENESS.

It is a cruel taskmaster because it is unrelenting in its emotion and physical beatings, leaving permanent scars and damage IF left unchecked.

My wife and I knew forgiveness was inevitable and as true Christians possessing the spirit of God (love), forgiveness was not even a second thought but rather a first-nature response. We came together, discussed what occurred, how we each felt, and how we were going to move on by using the POWER of forgiveness.

I use the word POWER because that is exactly what it is, a force of God that gives us the strength to do what we naturally do not want to do nor what we are naturally capable of doing alone.

Forgiveness is a force, strength, a GRACE, given by God to free yourself of antagonizing, debilitating feelings, negative emotions, and of the physical changes that accompany forgiveness, which we will discuss later in the book. You must receive it to give it to give it.

Once Amichia and I released the Power of Forgiveness, we began to receive newness in our home. We did not realize how much that particular wrongdoing or rather our failure to forgive, had adversely affected the atmosphere are home, other relationships, etc. This is what we discussed earlier, *the forgiving of the person not the natural act* that really did occur.

The act (lack of repayment or communication) did occur. There is no denying that. It is something that cannot be undone. It did occur BUT it should not continue to dwell in us, living out in our daily lives in some form or fashion.

Remember this simple but powerful statement:

"We cannot undo the past but we can change

its effect on our future by not allowing it to adversely affect us in any way."

Dr. Antonio B. Jones

We forgave the individuals although we never really heard from them again and definitely learned from that particular situation. Now, just like God our Father, He will ensure that you have truly forgiven at times by allowing you to see individuals you have forgiven. This is exactly what happened to us on several different occasions. We saw these individuals, had extensive conversations with them, etc. but did not mention the entire money thing to them because we were FREE. Yes, FREE!! The POWER of forgiveness was manifested and this particular process was complete. We had passed this particular test!! Glory to God! We chose POWER over PAIN!

Now, did the enemy AND my natural mind bring it up internally? Yes, it did. This again, is the nature of our flesh and carnal minds. I had to "will" or choose not to follow the script that was playing out in my head to address the act of offense. I had already forgiven them and as a family, we had moved on. Again, did the wrongdoing exist? Of course it did. Was I denying that the wrongdoing occurred or acting as if it never occurred? No. I simply <u>CHOSE</u> (willed myself) to continue to walk in forgiveness, true love, so that my family and I could remain free.

"You see, forgiveness is often continual, progressive in nature. It is not simply GOING to happen just because you WANT IT to happen, you must MAKE it happen."
Dr. Antonio Jones

I dare not given anyone or any situation that much power, authority and influence over my family, our feelings, emotions, etc. I had to make a conscious, informed decision, not based on my feelings, emotions, or what "I" wanted, but rather with my spiritual mind, so as to walk in love and to keep my family free from the chains and fetters of unforgiveness. Oh how liberating it felt to do so!

God loves us so much that He wants us to truly be free and walk in true agape love, demonstrating it by our interactions with everyone. We are commanded to LOVE EVERYONE, not because of, but INSPITE of. Exercising the power of forgiveness is one way that allows us to do this. You just have to cooperate fully with the spirit and then choose or will yourself to do so.

This single experience led me to really ask God to bless us financially so that if HE directed us to give again, which was inevitable, it would be a GIFT. Simply meaning, we would be able to give per His unctioning and not expect it back. WOW! This came simply out of our willingness to sincerely forgive AND receive the manifold reasons behind this incident aka blessing. We desired to be blessed so that we could BE a blessing; to be LENDERS not borrowers.

So once we forgive, we should always accept the lessons learned, apply them, and look for ways to prevent such things from occurring again, when possible.

Now let's go back to Matthew 18:23-35. These scriptures speak of an unforgiving man. The passage says:

> The Message (MSG)

23-25 "The kingdom of God is like a king who decided to square accounts with his servants. As he got under way, one servant was brought before him who had run up a debt of a hundred thousand dollars. He couldn't pay up, so the king ordered the man, along with his wife, children, and goods, to be auctioned off at the slave market.

26-27 "The poor wretch threw himself at the king's feet and begged, 'Give me a chance and I'll pay it all back.' Touched by his plea, the king let him off, erasing the debt.

As stated earlier, forgiving individuals as it relates to money is one area that many struggle with simply because we really do not possess the FULL MEASURE of the love of God.

 Let me say it like this, MONEY HAS A LOT OF US, WE DO NOT HAVE MONEY!! Glory to God!

That is a revelation in and of itself. In reality, <u>WE</u> SHOULD HAVE MONEY, MONEY SHOULD <u>NOT</u> HAVE (control) US! Let us strive to shift to the latter.

Now, I say the aforementioned because if the full measure of God's love in us, we would easily realize

that money is a small thing in the eyes of God. It is His money that He gives to us, allows us to obtain & to be good stewards over. It is a replaceable commodity. It is more where that came from.

The love of God is thereby placed before a love of money. In short, let NOTHING separate you from the love of God (Rom.8:37-39).

Well, I hear in the spirit that someone is saying, "Well I work hard for my money and cannot afford to waste it by forgiving a debt that has been around for a long time, even if it's a close friend or family member." This, friends, is totally untrue.

Some things are simply just not worth you losing sleep over, diminishing your quality of life over, or even worth remaining upset about. Many times forgiveness and a change in decision-making go hand in hand.

We simply have to **FORGIVE & LIVE™** (official workshop series by Dr. Antonio Jones). Yes, it is a process, which is one of the reasons the books in this FORGIVENESS series are not hundreds of pages each.

Forgiveness can take **time** to fully embody, process, and apply consistently. It forgiveness an experience? Yes! Does this mean it can happen instantly? Yes! Is forgiveness sometimes something one methodically goes through initially? YOU BET! This book series is a tool to assist you in that process, one book at a time, written in short increments to help with its application.

Now just as the king in the scripture was moved by the servant's plea had compassion and forgave his debt, so it is with us. The key factor here is when we ask for forgiveness we must ensure that we are sincere. This is demonstrated by an OBSERVABLE BEHAVIOR CHANGE.

The king forgave the servant thereby relieving himself (the king) of one additional thing to worry about and to potentially rob him of additional peace in his life. Ask yourself do you honestly need anything else to think about?

Let us continue. The next verses read:

²⁸ "The servant was no sooner out of the room when he came upon one of his fellow servants who owed him ten dollars. He seized him by the throat and demanded, 'Pay up. Now!'

²⁹⁻³¹ "The poor wretch threw himself down and begged, 'Give me a chance and I'll pay it all back.' But he wouldn't do it. He had him arrested and put in jail until the debt was paid. When the other servants saw this going on, they were outraged and brought a detailed report to the king.

³²⁻³⁵ "The king summoned the man and said, 'You evil servant! I forgave your entire debt when you begged me for mercy. Shouldn't you be compelled to be merciful to your fellow servant who asked for mercy?' The king was furious and put the screws to the man until he paid back his entire debt. And that's exactly what my Father in heaven is going to do to each one of you who doesn't forgive unconditionally anyone who asks for mercy."

Does not the latter part of this scripture speak volumes? Does it not maybe remind us of how we once were? Still are? Immediately after the servant asks forgiveness and was given his reprieve, he goes out and fails to provide mercy or forgiveness to one that has offended him through an owed debt.

He not only failed to demonstrate the love of God thru forgiveness that he was given by the king, he failed to remember how the king's forgiveness relieved him of a burden or worrisome situation. To add insult to injury, the amount that the servant was forgiven was much greater than what his fellow servant owed him.

What is God saying? How can we ask Him for forgiveness of things we have done, said, etc. to others and then not receive the apology or request for forgiveness we receive from others? This is extremely hypocritical.

** Review Matthew 6:12, 14-15 to assist in the processing the aforementioned, with specific emphasis on verse 15.**

You see, we often look at what someone has done and how much it hurt us, offended or affected us and decide that we can NEVER forgive the individual based on the pure act itself. No matter how treacherous, how conniving, how undermining the act committed against you was, it is a forgivable act. Let me repeat that, it is forgivable. Well, Dr. Jones, you just do not understand how deep the offense was and how close the person and I were. There is just NO way I can I forgive them.

Well, if that truly be the case, there is NO WAY God can forgive your offenses according to the end of the following passage that you just read; *"And that's exactly what my Father in heaven is going to do to each one of you who doesn't forgive unconditionally anyone who asks for mercy."*

Notice the word *unconditionally.* True forgiveness does not have strings attached, conditions place on it, nor does it set parameters in which forgiveness can occur. There is no power in this type of forgiveness. There is no true release in this type of forgiveness. This is exactly why we ALL need Christ and the love of God to help us. We are not able to forgive on that level in and of ourselves. Attempting to do so will be futile and lead to frustration and the desire to abandon the entire notion of forgiveness.

Conditionally forgiving still robs you of a quality of life, well-being, etc., that you were created and have a spiritual legal right to have. It steals the true peace that passes all understanding given only by Jesus Christ (Phil.4:7). Unforgiveness sets the stage for continually bitterness to ravage your life, your mind, and those who had nothing to do with the act that initially offended you. Not only is it not fair to you, it is not fair to those around you.

Please be aware that this is exactly what the enemy wants you do to, superficially forgive. This is, again one of the reasons why the enemy uses issues relating to money or finances to cause seemingly unforgivable offenses.

According to I Timothy 6:10, the <u>LOVE</u> of money is the root of all evil (not <u>having</u> a lot of money). It is usually this misplaced love that tries to prevent one from forgiving. We cannot love money more than our fellow man. No matter how important money is, no matter much or how little you may have of it, it does NOT supersede the LOVE OF GOD that is to be demonstrated towards our fellow brothers and sisters.

As a matter of fact, the more MONEY you have, the more LOVE you are commanded to share. This means giving, sharing, doing things to assist mankind while you are enjoying the fruit of your labor as well.

I am personally sharing in this particular volume of the FORGIVENESS Series to let you know that you are NOT the only individual that may be dealing with or that has dealt with forgiveness as it relates to money or finances. You see, there is a lot more that we all have in common, regardless of race, gender, ethnicity, etc., that what we realize.

We must learn to embrace these similarities that we share instead of focusing on the differences, so that we can help each other through difficult and trying times. This is extremely important if we desire to reduce the frequency of preventable acts of offense that will eventually lead to forgiveness.

Now let's look at another practical example.

My wife and I were looking to purchase a vehicle earlier in our lives and we came to know of an individual who was referred by a pastor acquaintance. This person was a car broker, locating and selling cars that his customers would request. As usual, we did our research on this individual and found that they had a good track record as it related to conducting sound, legitimate and legal transactions, even working with major dealerships.

In fact, a lot of the deals we had feedback on were excellent. This was aside from the fact that this person was highly recommended by this particular pastor. So needless to say we went ahead and began business transactions with this individual.

We were instructed that the vehicle we were looking for was found and were sent the pictures, dealership information, and pricing details, including payments, etc. The individual informed us that the local dealership usually used to bring the car here was requesting a few hundred dollars to secure a driver to get the car and bring it back to the dealership. Again, no initial red flags went up because of the individuals who referred the person to us had highly recommended him and they had proof of such purchases.

To make a long story short, the individual never made good on their promise for delivery of the car and upon contacting the dealer, it was disclosed that the person was indeed working there but only per a recent court orders to pay back debts for doing some other customers the same way.

Yes, we were livid and felt betrayed not only by the individual, but by the individuals who referred the person due to the fact that they were in contact with this person almost on a daily basis due to other obligations. The salesperson never returned calls nor did the individuals who referred us, until we threatened legal action.

Here lies the purpose of what I am saying. We never received any of the money back and felt betrayed by them as well as the salesperson. Months later, I finally was able to speak with the salesperson and literally went off on the person. I did not curse as I do not use such language but I definitely explained very vivaciously how we felt, what it had done, and how the entire ordeal was handled by both this individual and the respected person that referred him.

I did not give any time for a rebuttal or any other works and simply hung up the phone. Did I feel justified? YES! Did I initially feel liberated for getting that off my chest? Did I feel like "the man?" You better believe it! After all, they had it coming and I was finally going to be free of that mess, or so I thought.

Now did this last? Unfortunately, no it did not. You see, God is so graceful and merciful to us that He expects us to do the same.

God, being the God that He is in my life, simply said in a loving manner,

"Antonio, that was good that you were able to share with him what & how you felt. It was good that you were able to relieve yourself of that burden. It was good that you openly shared your disappointment in the salesman and the person who referred you. Now, if you REALLY want to continue in that pattern, call that person back and ask for forgiveness."

Wait, stop the presses! I felt like Arnold from the old sitcom Different *Strokes,* who often asked the proverbial question, *"What you talking about Mr. Willis"* or in my case, "What you talking about GOD!"

I honestly could not believe what I had just heard. Yes, I said heard because I knew God's voice but yet the words that He expressed to me had me dumbfounded and was not something my flesh wanted to hear yet alone receive. To ask this person for forgiveness when they were the one that committed the offense seemed far-fetched, even for God. I just could not believe it!

I then started my ***soulish justification*** *(another book series by Dr. Jones)* as to why I should not have to do this. I was in awe! Here we were out of hundreds of dollars, fighting bouts of anxiety and feelings of wanting to cause physical harm to someone and God is saying ask them for forgiveness.

I know some of you are looking at the last statement made and are asking yourselves how could this pastor, an Apostle of God, have felt like harming someone. Simply put, we are ALL humans, with real feelings, emotions, and "natural" responses. The thing is, many leaders rarely admit that they/we are tempted with these feelings often and can become even m ore effective and relatable by sharing such things at times. Yes, we are to practice what we teach/preach and what leaders share, we have to bear ourselves, thereby becoming first partakers of what is being released to others.

Such things mentioned above do still come to the mind of even the most mature Christians BUT the different is once such thoughts come, we cast them down. If we do not cast such thoughts down, they have a tendency to fester and possible become a reality, with real results. This is not the righteousness of God so I had to cast down and destroy those feelings anytime the enemy and my mind tried to bring it up.

My OLD nature had died and I could not allow anything nor anyone to re-construct & then resurrect him.

So after my laundry list of why I should not have to ask forgiveness was presented to God, He then presented me His reason behind the commandment. Did I say commandment? Yes, it was a commandment, not a SUGGESTION.

God told me this, *"Antonio, you had every right to share with the individual what you did and I am proud of you for doing so. What was not good was the manner in which you did it. It was not in love nor was it truthfully for the benefit of helping that person better themselves. You do not want to dilute your witness through your mannerisms as it relates to verbal communication. It was not WHAT you said; it was HOW you said it and your true MOTIVE behind it. Now make the call."*

I had to immediately repent and ask God to forgive me. I hear some of you saying that you still do not get why I was asked to ask for forgiveness when I received the "wrong end of the stick." That is simple, to whom much is given, much is required. God had placed a great ministry work in me and I could not allow something so menial to affect it. I could not allow my good to be ill-spoken of. Talk about humbling oneself!

This my friends, was one of the hardest things I had to "will" myself to do. It was truly genuine and beneficial, although it did not appear to be such on the surface. I know this baffles many people but it still does not remove this responsibility. Long story short, I did not have a choice in the matter. I am charged, as true believers are, to represent God (who is Love) at all times and whenever that does not occur, amends must be made.

Did this make me a bad person? Of course not. Does it mean that it would not occur again? Of course not. What it does mean is that I was now more aware of such things possibly occurring and have a greater propensity and responsibility to reduce and/or eliminate them. I learned from my mistakes by ensuring I did not make them again.

I made the call and the person was amazed, actually admitting that they should be the one apologizing for the incident(s) and how it was handled. I asked and received the forgiveness and actually informed the individual that we were forgiving him as well. God also allowed for a word of wisdom and a word of knowledge to be shared with the individual to include, but not limited to, the re-purposing of their gifts, talents, and energy into more productive things so as to help people and improve their own self-worth & self-esteem.

Remember this,

"You do not have to UNDERSTAND to obey."

Dr. Antonio Jones

The unfortunate part of this story is that this individual was truly gifted and naturally had a mind for business and could have been a very wealthy individual, assisting many individuals and building the kingdom of God, if it had not been for a lack of moral character, integrity, and honesty as it related to business and relationships in general. Skillsets, gifts, and talents ALONE will not make you success. Your CHARACTER and INTEGRITY will always take center stage.

A quote from my **POWER OF CHARACTER** book emphasizes the aforementioned;

"Your gifts (talents) may get you ON the stage, but your CHARACTER will KEEP you there..."

Dr. Antonio Jones

You see, the actual LOVE of money materialized in this person's life and when you love something or someone, you go to extremes to please that person or obtain that particular thing.

This downward spiral in this individual's life continued as they failed to forgive themselves for the many other similar acts committed. This not only caused the individual to continue to make bad decisions but led to them to not correct the behavior(s) that others had already forgave them of. This is why forgiveness is a personal act that starts with **YOU**, not the other person.

As stated in Volume I, the aforementioned demonstrates one aspect that your act of forgiveness has no role in. A person has to <u>commit</u> to behavior change, with or without you forgiving them.

Forgiving allows you to move on and releases any negative effect the other person may have had on your life, whether directly or indirectly. In short, you forgive and move on. Without this occurring, one will remain in the inevitable cycle of destruction rendered by unforgiveness. Remember, unforgiveness is that cruel taskmaster that attempts to "work" you to death.

Lastly, along with forgiving this person, we also had an obligation to pray for them, others that may have fell to these scams, and even the businesses, individuals, churches, etc., they may have had dealing with, with the hopes that there would be a measurable behavior change that would benefit this individual.

Again, throughout the entire process, this person's behavior did not change, even with numerous opportunities to "make things good." The individual just simply failed to do so.

Was this alone enough for us not to forgive what the person had done against us and the others who likely preceded us? NO!

Was it difficult doing so? YES! Was it still necessary? YES! There is NOTHING too hard for the Lord.

This is why we NEED Him in every aspect of our act of forgiveness.

It was "naturally" unthinkable that this person, who was highly recommended, would do such a thing. We had to allow God to deal with them while we totally forgave the person. The laws of the land would effectively deal with the rest. Talk about a growing pain! This was definitely one to grown on.

Again, we were committed to not allow money to rob us of our sanity, peace, and quality of life that God provided for us, something we admonish you to do as well.

God directed me to share just a few real-life examples to let you know that you are not undertaking the process of forgiveness by yourself.

<u>YOU ARE NOT ALONE</u>! We all have experienced and will continue to experience such things.

Part of my God-given responsibility is to provide a means to that end, through effective teachings of His revealed Word and HIS LOVE.

Everyone at some point or another has experienced a situation or circumstance involving money that required forgiveness on some level.

Money is dear to many of us so again, what better way to create division between two or more individuals than to involve it in the offense.

The enemy is on his job, so we too must be on ours, countering every move he attempts to cause divisions amongst our fellow brothers and sisters.

We must be committed to the fact that:

"MONEY DOES NOT HAVE US,

                                   WE HAVE MONEY"!

                                           Dr. Antonio B. Jones

In doing so, forgiveness within the area of money & finances will come easier. I challenge you to be purposeful and very intentional in your desiring to forgive. The scripture tells us to be diligent and steadfast in that which we do. This is the only way that the POWER of forgiveness can be fully released in your life.

PHYSICAL MANIFESTIONS OF UNFORGIVENESS

Have you heard of the old cliché:

"You are what you eat?"

Even though contrite and possibly overused, there is some truth to this saying.

All too often many of us eat of the raw indignation served by unforgiveness, even going back for seconds because we have made ourselves immune to its bitter aftertaste. When we fail to forgive, we become victims of just that.

We often become immune to the side-effects and the sour and unpleasant taste that accompanies unforgiveness because the innate desires of our flesh deceive us into thinking it is the exact opposite.

Our flesh tells us that the taste is good and whatever will be will be so there is no need for you to attempt to loose the very thing(s) that have kept you bound for so long and that have secretly manifested themselves in the form of physical ailments.
 This is why we must now take a look into some physical manifestations that unforgiveness can involve.

Many of us do not ever consider or even take the time to think about how failing to forgive can affect our physical bodies. We cannot begin to fathom the idea that our physical bodies can sometimes be the unfortunate recipients of our unwillingness to forgive others and/or ourselves. It does not seem logical to us but it is a true reality nonetheless.

When we do not forgive, we often experience such things as anxiety, depression, extreme anger accompanied by increased blood pressure, headaches, migraines, increased urination or bowel movements just to name a few.

We often "blow" these things off and do not equate them with being a by-product of unforgiveness. I can tell you firsthand; these are sometimes the result of failing to forgive. Do not take my word alone for this.

I encourage you to search the internet for forgiveness and physically manifestations of not doing so. I guarantee that you will be <u>extremely</u> surprised at what you find to include, but not limited to, medical research & studies, to say the least, supporting what I am sharing about the relationship between failing to forgive & certain physical manifestations. An amazing but not surprising trend can easily be identified in all of them.

All of these studies are not included in this particular volume as some are discussed during the **FORGIVE & LIVE™** sessions .

Nevertheless, I want to make you aware of this unhealthy relationship to further encourage you to begin & continue your process of learning to forgive. So, now let me show you how real this relationship is by sharing some information from some well-respected sources.

According to an article in the January issue of *Harvard Women's Health Watch*, forgiving those who hurt you can improve your mental and physical wellbeing.

The HARVARD HEALTH PUBLICATION (Dec. 2004) states," It may come as a surprise that forgiving is a skill you can hone, and that granting forgiveness may actually do more for you than the person you forgive. . . It was also found that mentally nursing a grudge puts your body through the same strains as a major stressful event: Muscles tense, blood pressure rises, and sweating increases. . ."

"Power of Forgiveness: Forgiving Others." *Harvard Health Publications.* 2004 Dec. Web. Jan 2014. (http://www.health.harvard.edu/press_releases/power_of_forgiveness)

Here you see how Harvard scientifically studied to show that the following five (5) positive health benefits could be achieved through forgiving:

- ❖ REDUCED STRESS
- ❖ BETTER HEART HEALTH
- ❖ STRONGER RELATIONSHIPS
- ❖ REDUCED PAIN
- ❖ GREATER HAPPINESS

These, and other studies, just prove exactly what can be found in the scriptures; unforgiveness is UNHEALTHY & forgiveness is something you can actually work on and improve upon.

In addition, forgiveness is scientifically encouraged. So, we now know God says about forgiveness in the scriptures, what the scientific community says about forgiveness, so now I must ask one question.

WHAT DO "YOU" now say about the POWER of FORGIVENESS?

Your own additional personal search of this subject will also become more meaningful to you if you are the one to see the plethora of articles discussing the relationship between failing to forgive and manifestations of sickness, illness, and/or disease. Do not view them from your clouded perspective bought about by an unwillingness to forgive and/or an unwillingness to accept the adverse relationship between some physical ailments and unforgiveness. As my sons used to often say,

"IT IS WHAT IS IT!"

In addition, many may not even be aware that

unforgiveness is still being harbored in them even though some of these physical manifestations are present. We just do not put the two together because after all, we are in control right? We are educated and know better right? We are "right" with God so there is no way this could happen to "ME!"

I mean we are strong, independent thinkers and would never allow such a thing or person to affect us to the point where it physically affects us! After all, we know our bodies right? We live in a technologically savvy world and there mere "thought" of not forgiveness affecting us is nonsense, maybe even heresy, right? Anything that is or would adversely affect or effect us, our physicians and/or other applicable professionals would be able to diagnose so that would definitely rule out unforgiveness, right? While we are most appreciative of the medical & psychological community, there are some things a physical or mental exam will not be able to identify.

This is where YOU come into play. Just like we give medical histories upon being examined, you must present an honest "history" per se of things you may still be holding on to that fall within the realm of unforgiveness. Yes, there is such a thing as **"generational unforgiveness"** which we will discuss in the next volume.

In short, this is no different than your medical histories seemingly travelling from generation to generation. If you have consistently been exposed to an unwillingness to forgive throughout your years of life, you are likely unaware that this "spiritual influence" has migrated in your generation without you even being aware. We have seen this time and time again, individuals desiring to forgiving but are unable to do so alone because of this very thing deceptively manipulating them not to do so. Again, we will discuss **"generational unforgiveness"** in future volumes.

Naturally speaking, and under normal circumstances, we would definitely never give someone or something that type of POWER or CONTROL over us. It is just not worth it and besides, we pride ourselves in being to intelligent for that. Hmm, we often say what we do not practice even though our intents may be well-purposed.

Is the <u>process</u> of forgiving now beginning to make even more sense? Are you beginning to identify some areas of your life that now have the fingerprints of unforgiveness smudged on them? This is one reason why God instructed me to continue to take the FORGIVE & LIVE™ sessions all over the world. It provides a safe place to discuss issues, problems, etc., that keep so many in bondage and allows them to "jumpstart" their forgiveness process amongst others who care, who are going through similar situations, all while being positively influenced & encouraged to continue on their "journey" to FORGIVENESS.

Remember, acknowledgement of harboring unforgiveness is one the foundational things we must do in order to even BEGIN the process of forgiving.

In short, failing to forgive can and will lead to certain outward manifestations that can adversely affect your well-being. The spiritual evidence and the physical evidence is there, again, along with the scientific community openly acknowledging this.

I say that to say this, we can no longer physically or emotionally afford to allow unforgiveness to degrade our bodies, minds, and relationships. It is time to continue to move forward and take back the quality of life, peace of mind, and physical well-begin God intended us to have.

To bring this point home, just take a few moments to recall a time where you did not forgive. What did you feel? How did you feel? Did you find heart racing whenever you say or heard the person? Did you feel the blood racing through your veins whenever you recalled the situation and/or person?

Did you withdraw yourself for extended periods of time consistently after an offense? Where you experiences changes within your physical body in any of the aforementioned circumstances and situations? The likely answer is a resounding YES!

Many of us, if not all of us, have experienced these feelings after an offense (forgiveness here since this is the subject matter of this book).The point here is that continual unforgiveness can put you at greater risk of experiencing these types of manifestations more frequently than you normally would.

So, then, I have to ask. What individual in their right state of mind would continue down a destructive, debilitating road KNOWING what was ahead and what would happen? GET OFF THIS ROAD NOW!

So, still not convinced of the correlation between failing to forgive & physical manifestations? Let's look further into this with a case study as you also continue to conduct your own personal research via internet & other means.

MARY

My wife and I conduct **FORGIVE & LIVE™** Seminars all over the world and for all types of individuals, groups, and various organizations. One of these sessions was conducted some years ago with an older woman who had experienced what she related to an unforgiveable offense. This offense was perpetuated by a close relative and a close "friend." I will refer to this woman by the fictitious name of Mary.

To curtail my example, let's say the offense basically equated to Mary being talked about in a very demeaning manner, attacking her integrity and character. As noted in my **Power of CHARACTER** book, I define character as "WHO YOU ARE" not what others SAY you are. It is who you are all the time, regardless of who is or is not around you. It is, my friends, THE <u>REAL</u> YOU!

Mary was initially informed about the conversations and what was said about her by a so-called confidante, who was Mary's relative. There was also another friend involved. Mary knew the information that she had received was accurate as she had the opportunity to overhear these same individuals basically having the same conversation again.

On one particular instance, Mary and the other two women were actually in a meeting together and what was once likely true speculation or hearsay now became truth as the two openly verbalized their previous thoughts about Mary.

This incident took Mary by surprise as it would many. To hear something from a third-party is always questionable at times, but to hear it from the primary person, aka "the horse's mouth," is another thing all together.

Well, Mary made up her mind that she would just not be able to forgive them, vowing within herself that she would fall into a self-induced doldrum, not speak what she knew she should say, thereby keeping the peace. Here is the dilemma:

> YOU WILL <u>NEVER</u> HAVE PEACE WITH UNFORGIVENESS IN YOUR HEART!!

Mary exhibited behavior that is very common after a hurt or offense. Instead of effectively and methodically working THROUGH the issue, we often permit the issue to work THROUGH us. The issue then becomes a cell-altering, body morphing, and mind-altering organism that begins eating away at us from the inside out that leads to some outward manifestations or behaviors.

With that being said, we then, just as Mary did,

begin to produce "fruit" of the root called unforgiveness. Fruit are those actions and behaviors that are produced by the seed of unforgiveness.

Let's take a look at Matthew 12:33 which states;

Either make the tree good, and his fruit good; or else make the tree corrupt, and his fruit corrupt: For the tree is known by his fruit.

The tree for what we are discussing is called unforgiveness, which grew from a small seed planted and allowed to grow inside us. It's that offense, that situation, that person, that wrong-doing that we just cannot shake. It lies inside of us, slowly growing and expanding into all parts of our very being and life, deceptively impacting our very actions and interactions.

It is like a cankerworm that is eating up all that is in site, being fed by things and words we often overlook and say without thinking about their potential impact on anyone or anything. This is one reason unforgiveness is so deadly. It is a proverbial sniper waiting for the right time to release a deadly shot that is intended to take you and others out.

It then begins to produce the fruit. Examples of these types of fruit include distrust of the opposite sex due to the "seed" planted from a jilted relationship and bitterness towards everyone due to the "seed" of a past disappointment, just to name a few. This is often the "seed" that allows "generational unforgiveness" to thrive undetected & unchallenged for years within one's lineage.

You see, these "fruit" are usually the only things people deal with but they are on a superficial level, albeit very real. These are the things, behaviors, etc., that are readily visible, from the outside and of which most people experience. We "deal" with these things, even, curtailing the frequency of which they manifest and then falsely believe that we have "overcome" the problem when in actually all we have done was

PRUNE THE TREE & LEFT THE SEED.

Mary's example shows this perfectly. She disassociated herself from the individuals among other things, which gave her a hiatus from interacting with the two women, but also produced the fruit of bitterness and reluctantly towards women.

This caused another fruit in the form of distrust and the delusion of people talking negatively about here whenever she had to engage in a meaningful dialogue with anyone.

The "seed" or the root cause of the problem, her unforgiveness, was left intact, with the innate ability to grow at an alarming rate in regards to multiplying its "fruit".

This is why, again, we must come to grips with the fact that our unwillingness to forgive does indeed affect us more than what we know and in more ways that we realize. Oftentimes, it is not just us that unforgiveness affects. Family members, co-workers, spouses, friends, and sometimes even strangers, are unintended victims of the "fruit" produced by failing to forgive. Its "fruit" feeds you until you begin to "like" the taste of it and ultimately create a desire to stay in unforgiveness.

"In regards to forgiveness, we must stop dealing with the FRUIT and start dealing with the ROOT."

Dr. Antonio Jones

Unforgiveness breeds unforgiveness, PERIOD. Hurt people, HURT People! Many erroneously believe that they can, alone, override the consequences of unforgiveness based on their pedigree, educational background, financial status, or even religious affiliation. This is so far from the truth. Seeds produce after their own kind. You have never seen an apple seed produce a harvest of oranges have you? Sounds crazy right? My point exactly...

We are finite beings and are not capable of forgiving without the spirit of God being in operation. This is impossible and the reason why many cannot ever forgive as they attempt to do so on their own. This was never intended from the beginning. We have a natural dependency on God and any attempt to override this will land us in the field of despair and frustration. It is again, simply IMPOSSIBLE to do forgive without God's assistance.

Our flesh (natural man) loves the fruit and other manifestations that unforgiveness brings. Our flesh naturally desires that we stay in a state of unforgiveness.
Our natural man loves the chaotic, emotional state that accompanies unforgiveness, but we must take steps daily to change this to the peaceful, loving state characterized by our spirit man. I feel an

unction from the spirit to paraphrase the Apostle Paul;

" *I know the spirit, the law,* the right thing to do but there is a war going on in my members. When I desire to do go, evil (nature of our flesh) appears and what I do not WANT to do, I find myself doing. It is no longer me that is doing it but the sin, the thing that I have not killed, died to, that is now doing it.
My spirit is at constant battle with my flesh. The proverbial good versus evil is there because my flesh is naturally sinful, not wanting to do the right thing. I have a desire to do the right thing but realized that I cannot do it alone.

I need God, I need help. Now there is another war coming against my mind, attempting to tell me to do wrong, stay wrong. Imprisoning me to the very thing I am attempting to escape from. No one can TRULY rescue me, deliver me but God through HIS SON JESUS CHRIST. I must have HIM to escape for good and to consistently win this battle, for it is a part of our natural lives. (Romans 7:14-25).

Glory to GOD!! See, YOU ARE NOT ALONE! This battle has been going on for centuries. It just requires us to relinquish our natural tendency to do it alone and to just depend on God through the Son Jesus Christ to assist us, but WITH OUR FULL COOPERATION. He cannot do it without you. God will not violate your PERSONAL WILL. You must allow Him into your heart and mind, as well as follow His instructions.

This is why we must begin and continue the process of forgiveness. The stress and other physical manifestations of unforgiveness are daunting and unrelenting. They will continue to go THROUGH you, your relationships, conversations, and every part of your very being until it reduces you to an unforgiving, bitter, and prideful mass of cells and skin, with an empty, black core being disguised through the purchasing of material things and other such coping mechanisms.

UNFORGIVENESS MAKE YOU UGLY.

The good news is that you can stop this now, immediately. Mary did just that. Upon our continual follow up with Mary, she was able to regain her self-worth, her confidence in her presentations and other interactions, and eventually forgiving of the two women.

Mary so embraced the process of forgiveness that she was able to successfully tell the two women that she forgave them, even apologizing for her actions against them. This left the two women in awe as to how Mary was able to do this, especially knowing what they had said about her and the issues it caused Mary.

This is nothing more than

THE
POWER
OF
FORGIVENESS
at work.

SOULISH JUSTIFICATION: A MAJOR HINDRANCE TO FORGIVENESS

Remember, what I just paraphrased concerning the war among your members? Part of the reason this war is so lengthy and dangerous is due to something I call **SOULISH JUSTIFICATION**. This is another volume of books within itself but let us review from Volume I what *soulish justification is.*

 This is a term GOD divinely revealed to me to begin using to explain certain behaviors exhibited by humans. It is simply a mechanism in which we use our feelings, situations, circumstances, past experiences, etc, to justify our actions and/or responses.

It is soulish because it deals with our feelings, emotions, etc. and not our spirit. Be sure to get my book on soulish justification for further insight on this.

Now our SPIRIT man would not allow this and actually leads us away from this type of reaction and into RESPONDING by the spirit in LOVE. Yes, in love. We always have the choice to override the spirit if we choose to do so and quite honestly, many of us do this routinely, based on soulish justification. But, however, I challenge you to apply (produce) fruits of the spirit *(Gal 5:22)* during these challenging times.

What are these "fruits of the spirit" you say? Well, I am glad you asked. I will gladly share them with you along with the "works" of the flesh according to *Galatians 5:16-23:*

Fruit of the Spirit:

1. LOVE
2. JOY
3. PEACE
4. LONGSUFFERING
5. GENTLENESS
6. GOODNESS
7. FAITH
8. MEEKNESS
9. TEMPERANCE (Self-Control)

Works of the Flesh:

1. ADULTERY
2. FORNICATION (sexual immorality)
3. UNCLEANNESS (impurities)
4. LASCIVIOUSNESS (lustful pleasures)
5. IDOLATRY
6. WITCHCRAFT (sorcery)
7. HATRED (hostility)
8. VARIANCE (quarreling, arguing)

9. EMULATIONS (ex. outbursts of anger)
10. WRATH (selfish ambitions)
11. STRIFE (friction, discord, bitter disagreements)
12. SEDITIONS (inciting to rebel)
13. HERESIES (dissention, division, not conforming to truth)
14. ENVYINGS (resentment, jealous, excessively desiring what another may have or is)
15. MURDERS
16. DRUNKENNESS
17. REVELLING (wild partying)
18. OTHER SINS LIKE THESE

There are **TWICE** as many "works" of the flesh than there are "fruit" of the spirit. Hmm, significant difference right?

Now you should begin to see how soulish justification can negatively influence a person.

Let me elaborate briefly. The fruit of the spirit are bought about by seeds placed in you through your relationship with God AND your walking out or living out, God's righteousness (not yours) in your daily life. The more your "sow" good seeds, habits, actions, words, etc., the more fruit you will produce. As you produce these fruit, say of gentleness, you SHARE them with others through interactions with them.

As you SHARE your fruit, individuals BITE per se, your fruit and ingest a seed, a lot of time unaware to them. So now they have a "seed" of gentleness planted in them and it begins to grown. Once it begins to manifest, it is then up to that particular individual to "feed" or "fertilize" it with actions and behaviors that are becoming of the fruit from which it came. Remember this simple fact, whetherspiritually or naturally, a

SEED PRODUCES AFTER ITS OWN KIND.

Now again we see how "seeds" of unforgiveness can produce **"generational unforgiveness"** very quickly and easily. Once a seed is planted, its there and will produce the exact "fruit" it came from UNLESS an intervention occurs that stops the continual transfer of these "seeds" from person-to-person or generation-to-generation.

Have you ever heard the saying, "He is just like his father, or she is just like her mother?" This is partly due to "seeds" being planted in the individual. What am I saying? Be careful what "seeds" you plant and how you may inadvertently "feed" them. In regards to forgiving, let us sow "seeds" of forgiveness that will allow for a person to foster and embody the process in order to produce healthier minds, bodies, and relationships.

Now, let's briefly discuss the "works" of the flesh.

A quick review of the "works" of the flesh would cause anyone to take a second glance. None of these manifestations of our flesh are good, but all are a natural part of our flesh. This is why we MUST embody God and receive Christ, so that we can overcome these things and produce "fruit."

Now you should be able to see more clearly why there is a "war" going in us, spirit versus flesh. These "fruit" and "works" are strikingly different and will yield very different results. Well, how does this all relate to the process of forgiving? Again, I am glad you asked and being the gentleman that I am, I am now obliged to answer.

Naturally our flesh desires to produce these "works" and some yield to these desires while others do not. But, however, just because all of these do not apply directly to you per se, they will attempt to manifest themselves continually in our lives in some form or another. Tied into these works is unforgiveness.

Unforgiveness causes bitterness, strife, uncharacteristic behavior to be exhibited, and even murder at times. Neither of these are beneficial to anyone but our flesh tells us that engaging in these "works" will yield a permanent and excellent feeling. This could not be so far from the truth. The truth is that these "works" are very much temporary and will cause more damage than before the "works" actually manifest.

This is why we must embrace the act of forgiveness. The scripture ends informing us that this list of "works" of the flesh is by no means exhaustive but goes on. Failing to forgive does not stop with just the particular incident or person, but it also goes on, impacting other aspects of your life in an attempt to get you to produce more "works" than "fruit", which will eventually destroy you spiritually, emotionally, physically, and mentally. The fruit of the spirit and the works of the flesh are discussed in more detail in the *SOULISH JUSTIFICATION book* series.

Lastly, the fruit of FAITH is needed in forgiving. One must believe and know, that GOD first forgave them for their sins and iniquities BEFORE they are truly able to offer and even receive forgiveness.

According to *Hebrews 11:1*, "*Now faith is the substance of things hoped for, the evidence of things not seen.*"

This is why you cannot always "see" the need for you to forgive or engage in meaningful dialogue with God and others. You are not going to "see" it but you must "receive" it. Through your unyielding believe, your faith will manifest producing a tangible result that will be your evidence.

Let me put this very simply since our natural minds attempt to fight this (faith) continuously. Recall a day or night where you have gone outside and felt a nice, cool breeze gently blowing in your face and hair. Remember how refreshing it felt. Now continue to look back at that particular time and recall how the wind "LOOKED." Was it round? Square? Dark? Light? Oh, you say you could not "SEE" it but you "KNEW" it existed or was there because you felt the effects of it. Hmm, this is how faith is. You KNOW its there and that it is operating even during times you do not "feel" it. What am I saying? I am simply stating that forgiveness is not always going to be something you "WANT" to do or even "FEEL" like doing, but it is something you must do.

You see, if one never repents or feels the need to ever repent, they are not operating in true faith. The latter is true because if one doesn't ever believe that they have done anything wrong, *(I John 1:8)* it is like they are saying they do not believe that Jesus had to die for our sins and therefore why believe in Jesus because there is no need for a Savior.

Remember, we do not always have to be the ones who committed the offense in order to forgive. If the situation is still impacting you (i.e., you constantly talk about it, feel intense anger when you see the person, etc.,), then you need forgiveness to occur in your life. Remember this,

DELIVERANCE IS YOURS FOR THE ASKING! After you ask in FAITH, RECEIVE IT!!

Simply put, if I have not sinned (did or thought anything wrong), I do not need someone (Jesus) to cover my iniquities. This is in direct contrast with the scripture as we ALL die daily to sin *(I Cor. 15:31)* It is a prideful state for any of us, regardless of our positions spiritually, naturally, etc. to sincerely believe that we never sin. Does not the Bible tell us that we were born into sin and shaped by iniquity *(Psalms 51:5)?* We just do not STAY there nor do we condemn ourselves so that we become sin conscious.

This is one reason why we must become NEW creatures <u>through</u> Jesus Christ. He re-shapes us, molds us into what He desires, not what we want. There is a big different between the two. When we become what He desires, we become like him, we become love, NOT PERFECT. Remember, you are accepting the fact that the act calling for forgiveness DID occur, but you are NOT accepting its negative affect on your life and well-being.

IT STOPS NOW!!

SINCE WE HAVE ESTABLISHED THAT

FORGIVENESS CAN SOMETIMES BE A PROCESS

FOR SOME, LET US REVISIT SOME OF THESE

ITEMS TO HELP US GAUGE OUR PROGRESS.

THE FOLLOWING PAGES

CONTAINS SOME QUESTIONS THAT WERE TO BE

ANSWERED FROM VOLUME I.

IF YOU DID NOT COMPLETE THE SERIES OF QUESTIONS FROM VOLUME I, IT IS HIGHLY RECOMMENDED THAT YOU DO SO.

1. *What fact or situation occurred during your childhood that you first became aware of unforgiveness? (a) Who did you see that did not forgive? (b) What were the situations surrounding the event? The purpose of this question is to show a correlation between learned behavior (thru observation & repeated exposure) & unforgiveness and how it molds your response to such situations later in life.*

2. *What specific action or situation occurred during your latter years involving unforgiveness?*

   *If there is more than one event involving unforgiveness, you should repeat these questions for each event as it will likely reveal a behavior patterns and demonstrate how the initial event had a significant role in how you dealt with subsequent events. *

3. *How did you deal with the person(s) at that time? In other words, what was your reaction immediately? At a later date?*

4. Did *you* meaningfully attempt to resolve the issue? If so, how? If not, why?

5. Now, that you have time to begin exploring your specific situation(s), how do you feel now? (Be honest with your response as this is the only way to continue to walk in forgiveness)

6. What was the ultimate deciding factor(s) that made you decide to not forgive that person and/or those individuals?

I NOW RECOMMEND THAT AT SOME POINT IN THE VERY NEAR FUTURE, YOU REVISIT YOUR ANSWERS FROM YOUR VOLUME I BOOK, PAYING CLOSE ATTENTION TO THE "FEELING" OR "TONE" OF YOUR ANSWERS.

FOR THE LAST PART OF THIS PARTICULAR VOLUME, YOU WILL NEED TO COMPLETE THE FOLLOWING SET OF QUESTIONS AFTER DOING THE AFOREMENTIONED.

THIS WILL ALLOW YOU TO SEE HOW YOU ARE WORKING THROUGH THE PROCESS OF FORGIVENESS AND HOW FAR YOU HAVE PROGRESSED.

A. DOES THE FIRST SET OF ANSWERS FROM VOLUME I NOW SEEM MORE CRITICAL, HARSH, FULL OF HURT, OR EVEN WITH TONES OF HATRED? EXPLAIN.

(cont.)

B. WHAT FEELING(S) DID YOU EXPERIENCE OR NOT EXPERIENCE WHEN YOU ANSWERED THE QUESTIONS THE SECOND TIME? BE SPECIFIC.

_____
_____
_____
_____
_____
_____
_____
_____
_____
_____
_____
_____
_____
_____
_____
_____
_____
_____

(cont.)

C. WHAT FEELING(S) DID YOU EXPERIENCE OR NOT EXPERIENCE WHEN YOU ANSWERED THE QUESTIONS THE SECOND TIME? BE SPECIFIC.

_____
_____
_____
_____
_____
_____
_____
_____
_____
_____
_____
_____
_____
_____
_____
_____
_____
_____

(cont.)

D. USING A SCALE FROM 1-5, WITH 1 BEING THE HIGHEST LEVEL, HOW WOULD RATE YOUR FEELINGS OF PEACE & TRANQUILITY NOW OPPOSED TO WHAT YOU EXPERIENCE IN VOLUME I?

E. WHAT DO YOU CREDIT TO THE ANSWER ABOVE?

(cont.)

F. WHAT WILL YOU CONTINUE TO DO IN ORDER TO INCREASE YOUR RATING FROM QUESTION # D ABOVE?

_____
_____
_____
_____
_____
_____
_____
_____
_____
_____
_____
_____
_____
_____
_____
_____
_____
_____
_____

(cont.)

G. *NOW THAT YOU KNOW THAT THERE IS A RELATIONSHIP BETWEEN UNFORGIVENESS &SOME AILMENTS (A) HOW LIKELY ARE YOU TO ENGAGE IN FORGIVENESS? (B)WHAT SPECIFIC THINGS WILL YOU DO IN THIS REGARD?*

_____
_____
_____
_____
_____
_____
_____
_____
_____
_____
_____
_____
_____
_____
_____
_____
_____
_____
_____
_____
_____
_____
_____

(cont.)

(cont.)

H. IN THIS VOLUME WE DISCUSSED PHYSCIAL RESPONSES STEMMING FROM NOT FORGIVING. (A) BRIEFLY DISCUSS YOUR INTERNET FINDINGS. . (B) BASED ON YOUR INTERNET SEARCH RESULTS REGARDING THE RELATIONSHIP OF UNFORGIVENESS AND PHYSICAL AILMENTS, DISCUSS YOUR FINDINGS & COMPARE IT TO WHAT YOU HAVE OR ARE CURRENTLY EXPERIENCING. (C) DID YOUR RESULTS SURPRISE YOU?

_____
_____
_____
_____
_____
_____
_____
_____
_____
_____
_____
_____
_____
_____
_____
_____

(cont.)

(cont.)

THE VISION PLAN

I. WRITE THE VISION, MAKE IT PLAIN.
   WRITE OUT THE STEPS YOU WILL TAKE TO
   MOVE YOU TOWARDS FORGIVING.

_____
_____
_____
_____
_____
_____
_____
_____
_____
_____
_____
_____
_____
_____
_____
_____

(cont.)

SCRIPTURES

Here is a listing of some scriptures from the *Forgiveness Devotional* that relate to forgiveness. I again encourage you to meditate these scriptures and seek God diligently for revelation as it pertains to you and your situation(s):

- ➤ 1 Kings 8:50 And forgive thy people that have sinned against thee, and all their transgressions wherein they have transgressed against thee, and give them compassion before them who carried them captive, that they may have compassion on them:
- ➤ 2 Chronicles 7:14 If my people, which are called by my name, shall humble themselves, and pray, and seek my face, and turn from their wicked ways; then will I hear from heaven, and will forgive their sin, and will heal their land.
- ➤ Psalm 25:18 Look upon mine affliction and my pain; and forgive all my sins.

- Psalm 32:1 Blessed is he whose transgression is forgiven, whose sin is covered.
- Psalms 51
- Psalm 85:2 Thou hast forgiven the iniquity of thy people, thou hast covered all their sin. Selah.
- Psalm 86:5 For thou, Lord, art good, and ready to forgive; and plenteous in mercy unto all them that call upon thee.
- Psalm 103:3 Who forgiveth all thine iniquities; who healeth all thy diseases;
- Psalm 130:4 But there is forgiveness with thee, that thou mayest be feared.
- Psalm 130:4 But there is forgiveness with thee, that thou mayest be feared.
- Daniel 9:9 To the Lord our God belong mercies and forgivenesses, though we have rebelled against him;

- *Matthew 6:14 For if ye forgive men their trespasses, your heavenly Father will also forgive you
- *Matthew 6:15 But if ye forgive not men their trespasses, neither will your Father forgive your trespasses.
- *Matthew 18:21 Then came Peter to him, and said, Lord, how oft shall my brother sin against me, and I forgive him? till seven times?
- *Matthew 18:35 So likewise shall my heavenly Father do also unto you, if ye from your hearts forgive not every one his brother their trespasses.
- *Mark 11:25 And when ye stand praying, forgive, if ye have ought against any: that your Father also which is in heaven may forgive you your trespasses.
- *Mark 11:26 But if ye do not forgive, neither will your Father which is in heaven forgive your trespasses.

- *Luke 6:37 Judge not, and ye shall not be judged: condemn not, and ye shall not be condemned: forgive, and ye shall be forgiven:

(*KEY to true forgiveness)

- Acts 8:22 Repent therefore of this thy wickedness, and pray God, if perhaps the thought of thine heart may be forgiven thee.
- Acts 13:38 Be it known unto you therefore, men and brethren, that through this man is preached unto you the forgiveness of sins:
- Acts 26:18 To open their eyes, and to turn them from darkness to light, and from the power of satan unto God, that they may receive forgiveness of sins, and inheritance among them which are sanctified by faith that is in me.
- Romans 4:7 Saying, Blessed are they whose iniquities are forgiven, and whose sins are covered.

➢ 2 Corinthians 2:7 So that contrariwise ye ought rather to forgive him, and comfort him, lest perhaps such a one should be swallowed up with overmuch sorrow.

➢ 2 Corinthians 2:10 To whom ye forgive any thing, I forgive also: for if I forgave any thing, to whom I forgave it, for your sakes forgave I it in the person of Christ;

➢ Colossians 1:14 In whom we have redemption through his blood, even the forgiveness of sins:

➢ Romans 2:4 Or despisest thou the riches of his goodness and forbearance and longsuffering; not knowing that the goodness of God leadeth thee to repentance?

➢ 2 Timothy 2:25 In meekness instructing those that oppose themselves; if God peradventure will give them repentance to the acknowledging of the truth;

- Hebrews 6:1 Therefore leaving the principles of the doctrine of Christ, let us go on unto perfection; not laying again the foundation of repentance from dead works, and of faith toward God,
- Colossians 1:14 In whom we have redemption through his blood, even the forgiveness of sins:
- Colossians 2:13 And you, being dead in your sins and the uncircumcision of your flesh, hath

- he quickened together with him, having forgiven you all trespasses;
- James 5:15 And the prayer of faith shall save the sick, and the Lord shall raise him up; and if he have committed sins, they shall be forgiven him.
- 1 John 1:9 If we confess our sins, he is faithful and just to forgive us our sins, and to cleanse us from all unrighteousness.

This is by no means an exhaustive list of scriptures but just some to help you along your journey. I love the last verse as it speaks to what many of us have dealt with for years in regards to forgiveness,

FORGIVING YOURSELF.

Look again at the latter portion of I John 1:9. HE is faithful and just to forgive us…the HE is GOD. If GOD forgives us when we ask Him to, there is NO reason why we cannot (with His spirit in us) forgive ourselves.

Again, this is a device of the enemy to condemn ourselves over and over again to the point where we fall back into the unmerciful state of unforgiveness. But, my brothers and sisters, Roman 8:1 informs us:

There is therefore NOW NO condemnation to them which are in Christ Jesus, who walk not after the flesh, but after the Spirit.

Glory to the Lamb of GOD!! We thank God for His son and our Lord Jesus Christ, for the shedding of His blood for ALL of our sins, thereby enabling us to forgive ANYONE that offends us.

One of our goals is to DAILY repent of any wrongdoings, thoughts, etc., by simply asking God to forgive us and then making a conscious effort (by His Spirit dwelling in us) to not repeat those offenses against Him.

Will this always be easy? No. Is it necessary? Yes. Can we do it? Yes, for Mark 10:27 informs us that ..._with GOD, ALL things are possible..._

Remember,

"You cannot TRY forgiveness, you must COMMIT to it..."

Dr. Antonio Jones

PRAYERS

Let's continue our journey to total forgiveness by praying these simple but powerful prayers & confessions daily or as led by the Spirit of God:

My Father, which art in Heaven, hallowed be thy name. I come before you today with singing, thanksgiving, and praise. I ask in Jesus name, that according to your tender mercies that you blot out all my transgressions and wash me completely from my iniquities and cleanse me from my sins.

Pull down and utterly destroy every demonic stronghold, imaginations, and high thought that exalts itself against Your wisdom & knowledge and bring every thought captive to the obedience of Christ per II Cor.10:3-6.

Help me today & everyday, to be even more like You, to show more love towards everyone and to spread the Good News to everyone you have assigned me to.

Thank you for forgiving me for any wrong thoughts, attitudes, and responses that were not of You today and continue to help me as I do my part to help myself to better represent You. Thank you for forgiving me so that I can forgive others, and live a more productive life. In Jesus name, Amen.

Father, *I truly forgive everyone who has ever done me wrong, talked negatively about me, cursed at me, lied to me, betrayed me, spoken evil and wicked words over me, prayed witchcraft prayers over me and/or my family. I do not curse them, but bless them according to your word in Romans 12:14. I sincerely pray that these individuals seek You, find You, and accept You as their personal Lord & Savior, so that they too, can walk in forgiveness and love, and experience great peace. In Jesus name, Amen.*

I ask *that you to forgive me Father, for any anger, distrust, unforgiveness, bitterness, strife, bitterness, animosity, pride, and resentment that I have in my heart toward anyone or even myself now in Jesus name. With the help of your Spirit, I will now allow these things to adversely affect my life or that of my family again, in Jesus name, Amen.*

Father, I truly humble myself in complete repentance before you and ask that you cover my wrongdoings with the blood of Jesus. Create in me a clean heart, renew a right spirit in me. Don't take away your Spirit from me but restore me to the joy of Your salvation and uphold me so we can teach others and win souls for You. I appropriate your Blood and receive the benefits of GRACE that accompany it.

I thank you Father for this time with you and for doing all that I have asked in this prayer that is in alignment with Your Will, in Jesus name, Amen.

These are a just a few examples of prayers that you can utilize and implement within your own prayers or use to meditate on daily. The primary objective here is to steer you towards a personal, intimate, and continual dialogue with God.

Remember, you must start <u>somewhere</u> and prayer is an excellent place to begin. I encourage you to open yourself fully to God during your times of meditation and prayer, setting aside time specifically to spend with Him.

POINTS TO PONDER

Recall from Volume I that prayer is simply a sincere, honest dialogue between you and God. In that prayer, you are decreeing and agreeing with what He and His word (Bible) says about you and your situation(s). God desires you to COMMUNE with Him daily and has so much to share with us, <u>IF</u> we just take the time to TALK WITH HIM!!

Remember; don't talk so much that you are unable to hear when He speaks or desires to speak to you. Contrary to popular believe, God doesn't violate our will; we must willfully SUBMIT to His will to receive all that He desires for us.

I must again continue to KILL SACRED COWS (religious mindsets & beliefs that serve as hindrances to true relationship with God thru Jesus) by reiterating this:

You do **not** have to have a bunch of "thy arts", "thee", etc., in your prayer, nor do you have to spend hours on end (even though God may, on occasion ask this of you) in prayer saying a lot of "stuff" in hopes that God will hear you. Speak sincerely and candidly from the heart, for He already knows what is in us.

My point is this; God wants you to talk to Him just as plainly as you talk to another person, but with the respect to Him as the ONLY TRUE & LIVING GOD. Just remember to honor and reverence Him for who He is, God, the Father, your <u>ONLY</u> source, not just a RESOURCE.

I close this volume with these words;

"GOD DOESN'T DO RELIGION, HE DOES <u>RELATIONSHIP!</u>"

Dr. Antonio Jones

Religion is simply man's way & processes of reaching God. In short, we can't be *RELIGIOUS,* we must have *RELATIONSHIP* and *INTIMACY* with God that ONLY comes through His son JESUS CHRIST. Without it, forgiveness will remain an unobtainable reality.

God's way, which should be our way, is simply establishing & maintaining an intimate relationship with HIM, through prayer, devotion, worship, studying His word, and of course, accepting Christ as YOUR personal Lord & Saviour.

Yes, as you grow in Christ and study the Bible, you will learn how to decree & declare what God says (scriptures) in your prayers in order to be more effective in prayer and to be in spiritual alignment with His word & will through the GRACE He has already given us. This is homologeo (Greek) for confessing, saying, and believing what God said. You must develop a <u>LIFESTYLE</u> OF PRAYER. It is an ongoing process so God wants you to at least begin consistently talking to Him so that you can establish a prayer LIFE.

It's ok to say, for example, "God, I'm tired. I just do not know what to do and quite honestly, I do not even know what to even pray right now because I am so upset." What! We can talk to God that plainly? In simple terms? YES! If we possess the spirit of God, it will intercede for us in these times as we yield ourselves totally to it.

This is one of many reasons why He directed me in this season to begin releasing the books, manuals, devotionals, etc. He gave me some time ago, in a plain and simple manner, even if it meant not adhering to "industry standards." God said that's part of what has driven people away from Him, FORMALISM! LEGALISM! CONFORMING TO THE WORLD!

This is not meant to disregard order, process, or experience, but rather to re-emphasize total dependence and obedience to God, even if it means doing things some are not willing to do or being in the minority which is the majority if you are in GOD.

My sisters and brothers, I admonish you to just begin talking with God in your own way. He really does desire a meaningful relationship with you. You are on His mind. He yearns for you to tell Him what's hindering you from fully forgiving that person or yourself. He desires to help you but you must make the first step. Let me paraphrase Revelations 3:20;

Christ is standing at the door, knocking and when you hear His voice, Don't turn him away or leave Him waiting, OPEN THE DOOR & INVITE HIM INTO YOUR LIFE...

He is waiting to come into your life, fellowship with you, be your Father, Mother or whatever you need Him to be. You must, however, LET Him in. He will not force Himself upon you.

As always, I dare not conclude this writing without providing a scriptural reference for a prayer of repentance for those that do not know Jesus as their personal Lord & Savior.

When all else fails, and it is not a matter of IF something will fail, but WHEN, Jesus is still there. Won't you accept Him into your life and receive the GRACE that accompanies Him?

Contrary to popular and some religious beliefs, accepting Christ is really quite simple.

According to Roman 10:9, if <u>YOU</u> <u>CONFESS</u> with YOUR MOUTH the Lord Jesus AND <u>BELIEVE</u> in YOUR <u>heart</u> that God has raised <u>Jesus</u> from the dead, YOU shall be saved. You must SAY this from your own mouth & heart for this must be personal. Pastors, priests, ministers, your parents, spouse, organizations, etc., cannot do this for you.

Verse 10 further states that with the heart, men (you) believe unto righteousness and with your mouth confession is made unto salvation. It is that simple!!

Yes, I must say it again, *you do not have to roll over the floors, jump around, yell/shout out, etc. to receive Christ!* What you MUST do however, is to believe Jesus Christ IS the Son of God, that He died & rose again on the third day, and is now seated at the right hand of God the Father, interceding on our behalf.

So, what do you need God to do for you? Do you need peace, healing, or deliverance from past hurts?

Whatever it is, BELIEVE it, CONFESS it, and LIVE IT OUT LOUD! Allow the NEW YOU to win others over through your genuine expression of true love. Have NO FEAR & holdfast to your CONVICTIONS at ANY COST.

Although emotional and physical manifestations may occur with some people, which is totally ok, it is not a definitive characteristic of receiving Christ. You can accept God at home, in your car or even while reading this book. The true acceptance of Christ will then just be marked or followed by a measurable change in behavior, speech, belief, and lifestyle according to His written word and per the direction of His spirit dwelling in you.

JESUS is always there for you, calling you to COME… Will you hearken unto His call and receive Him today?

In closing, I again want to leave you with some words:

To continue your personal journey through forgiveness to healing, you must continue to face and overcome the very things, persons, and/or situations that you have intentionally chose not to, despite your natural/carnal mind directing you not to do so.

Recall from Volume I that this may be due to, but not limited to, the feelings associated with the situation, extenuating circumstances, or the person(s) involved being close to you. Whatever the reason, WILL yourself to overcome it by whatever means necessary as the Spirit of God leads you.
You have to want this more than anyone else. You must be willing to do whatever God instructs you to do in order to walk in total freedom and peace that can only come from being in Christ.

Next, remember to get to the **ROOT** of the issue(s) instead of dealing with just the *fruit* (symptoms or outward manifestations). As you continue to identify these fruit, consider how they have affected you since their occurrence and how they may even still affect you today.

Trace the fruit to the ROOT (cause) and begin uprooting it, replacing it with the love, etc., of God. I recommend you meditate *Matthew 15:13* which reads;

...Every plant, which my heavenly Father hath not planted, shall be rooted up.

God desires to rid us of that root of unforgiveness, etc., we just have to cooperate and allow Him to do it. So, will you receive this grace given to you by Christ?

Again, please continue to journal your thoughts on a daily basis as you continue in your daily meditations & prayer unto GOD. I recommend you that review your journal entries you began from Volume I as an aid to your faith, showing you the progress you have made thus far.

I know that some individuals may have even experienced forgiveness for a specific area or circumstance. You are commended on this achievement and I admonish you however, to not stop here. I encourage you to allow forgiveness to be an integral part of who you are and what you choose to do for the rest of your life.

Forgiveness is something that must be continually applied if it is to truly become a part of you. The seed of forgiveness has been planted, now it is up to YOU to cultivate it so that it becomes deeply rooted in you. Change is sometimes a process so continue to be intentional and methodical in incorporating your behavior changes in a consistent manner. For example, implement a "cooling off" period before responding to a situation whenever applicable, so as to allow for emotions and feelings to subside. This also allows you to seek God for guidance and His peace.

Reacting out of emotions usually amplifies the situation and usually makes matters worse as the likelihood that something is said or done that was not intended, greatly increases. Please know and realize that God is with you and will never forsake you.

Accept the true reality that NO ONE can forgive and then continue to walk in forgiveness alone. It takes the Spirit of God to do this but WITH your cooperation.

Choose to cooperate with the Spirit of God in order to walk in a more meaningful, liberated life; a life where other people or past situations are NOT in control of you, your responses, decision-making, how you love and treat individuals, or how you view God. Remember, God will NOT violate your freewill and will not go beyond what YOU allow Him to do.

Continue your process to daily development of your relationship with God systematically, personally and without unrealistic expectations & religious influence. FORGIVENESS is sometimes a process, so do not ever condemn yourself (Rom.8:1).

YOU CAN DO IT!!

As always, I am in your corner, cheering you on, encouraging you, praying for you, and believing that as you submit <u>ALL</u> to God, you will begin to experience Him in a manner you never thought possible and begin living & maintaining an increased quality of life (physically, mentally, and spiritually) once thought unreachable.

Let me reiterate, forgiveness can be immediate and it can also be A PROCESS!!

It ALWAYS takes GOD and it sometimes takes TIME!!

So let patience have her perfect work……..

NOW CELEBRATE YOUR PROGRESS THUS FAR AND STAY COMMITTED TO THE STATE OF CONSTANT FORGIVENESS, WITH ITS ACCOMPANYING PEACE, TRANQUILITY, AND INCREASED QUALITY OF LIFE!

MINISTRY INFORMATION

The FORGIVE & LIVE™ and the MAXIMIZING MARRIAGE™ workshops, seminars, and conferences are conducted by Drs. Antonio & Amichia Jones and can be bought to your city or country.

Please use the contact information provided for more information and scheduling on these and other specialized trainings and conferences.

*JMI International uses a portion of book sales to support its **DRIVE THE COMMUNITY (DTC)** Missions Ministry, which, at the time of this printing, focuses on, but not limited to, West Africa, Cote d'Ivoire. Visit the website to learn more about International Missions efforts.

www.jonesministries.org

JMI International was founded as an organization, not a denomination, for churches and ministries to come together as an alliance, to fulfill their highest calling to change the world through Christ.

JMI is designed to inspire and equip Christian leaders through the anointing of God with the tools to build Bible based churches and ministries that will impact the world.

The intent of JMI is to link faith- minded Believers together, empowered to fulfill the great commission and transfer the end-time harvest into the Kingdom of God.

JMI's purpose is:

1. To help empower JMI members in fulfilling the ministry and/or calling to which God has called them.

2. To provide an avenue for networking and fellowship among the JMI members.

3. To supply a vehicle through while JMI can share information and make available resources and training that will benefit JMI members in their pursuit of excellence in ministry and Kingdom building.

4. To establish a board from the ministerial alliance members, for the purpose of licensing, ordination, and especially ministry accountability.

5. To provide Biblically-based teaching and various ministry resources to equip church leaders and ministries to reach increasing numbers of unchurched people.

JMI is also home to the A.I.M.S. Bible Institute and School of Ministry, an accredited Bible College that teaches scriptural truths, trains ministers, and awards certificates as well as Associates thru Doctoral degrees.

The Global Teaching Network (GTN) provides individual and ministry specific trainings upon request. The latter is completed through conferences (i.e., marriage, leadership, etc.), revivals, programs, etc. Consultations are also provided upon request.

Dr. Antonio Jones & Dr. Amichia Jones serve as the President and Vice-President, respectively, of JMI's operations. They have been married for 16 yrs and are owners of the DRESS YOU UP® line of clothing boutiques. The Joneses are Spiritual Life Coaches and Community Advocates, who also provide ministry covering for ministries throughout the world, including the continent of Africa as well as the United States.

Please visit the website @ **www.jonesministries.org** for video clips, audio files, and other information, including a link to their weekly radio broadcast JMI LIVE: "It Starts With ME".

You can also join Drs. Antonio & Amichia Jones on **JMI LIVE** web channels (i.e., ROKU, USTREAM) Hearken Spiritual Television Network (HSTVN) in the US, UK, Australia and other countries. Tune in to **JMI LIVE** Radio Network (365 internet Radio), Fayetteville, NC.

Ministry/Speaking Requests for Dr. Antonio & Amichia Jones can be initiated by calling or email,but, however, an official letter/invitation must be mailed.

JMI INTERNATIONAL

P.O. BOX 8092

Fayetteville, NC 28311

www.ingramcontent.com/pod-product-compliance
Lightning Source LLC
Chambersburg PA
CBHW070948180426
43194CB00041B/1723